Professor Pete's Prehistoric Animals

SHARP-CLAWED DINOSAURS

W

FRANKLIN WATTS

LONDON • SYDNEY

Franklin Watts
This edition published in the UK in 2017 by The Watts Publishing Group

Copyright © 2013 David West Children's Books

Designed and illustrated by David West

ISBN 978 1 4451 5504 3

Printed in Malaysia

Franklin Watts
An imprint of
Hachette Children's Group
Part of The Watts Publishing Group
Carmelite House
50 Victoria Embankment
London EC4Y 0DZ

An Hachette UK Company.
www.hachette.co.uk

www.franklinwatts.co.uk

PROFESSOR PETE'S PREHISTORIC ANIMALS SHARP-CLAWED DINOSAURS
was produced for Franklin Watts by
David West Children's Books, 6 Princeton Court, 55 Felsham Road, London SW15 1AZ

Professor Pete says:
This little guy will tell you something more about the animal.

Learn what this animal ate.

Where and when (Mya=Millions of Years Ago) did it live?

Its size is revealed!

How fast or slow was it?

Discover the meaning of its name.

A timeline on page 24 shows you the dates of the different periods in Mya.

Burnt Ash Library
020 8460 3405

THE LONDON BOROUGH
www.bromley.gov.uk

https://capitadiscovery.co.uk/bromley
In partnership with

BETTER
the feel good place

Please return/renew this item
by the last date shown.
Books may also be renewed by
phone and Internet.

Contents

Austroraptor 4

Deinonychus 6

Gigantoraptor 8

Microraptor 10

Mononykus 12

Oviraptor 14

Therizinosaurus 16

Troodon 18

Utahraptor 20

Velociraptor 22

Glossary and Timeline 24

Austroraptor

aws-stroh-rap-tor

Like all raptors,
Austroraptor ran on two legs.
It had a killing claw which it
kept raised off the ground
when it ran or walked. This
claw was used to stab its **prey**.

Professor Pete says:
Austroraptor was one of the largest raptors. Its long jaws were filled with sharp teeth which it may have used to grab fish from lakes and streams.

Austroraptor means 'southern thief'.

Austroraptor could run up to 32.1 kilometres per hour.

Austroraptor was about 4.9 metres in length and weighed around 368 kilogrammes.

It lived in Argentina during the Upper Cretaceous period, 70 Mya.

Austroraptor was a meat eater and fed on plant eaters such as young titanosaurs. It may have eaten fish, too.

Deinonychus

die-NON-i-kuss

This active and agile **predator** hunted in packs. It attacked its prey by using its large stabbing claw while it held on with its clawed hands. Like many raptors its body was covered in feathers.

Deinonychus was a meat eater and it probably hunted dinosaurs that were much bigger than itself .

Deinonychus was not as fast as some raptors. It walked at 16.1 kilometres per hour and could probably run up to 40.2–48.3 kilometres per hour.

It lived in the United States during the Lower Cretaceous period, 120–110 Mya.

Deinonychus means 'terrible claw'.

Deinonychus grew up to 3 metres in length and weighed 59 kilogrammes.

Professor Pete says:
Deinonychus had a large brain for its size. This means it might have been quite intelligent.

Gigantoraptor

gee-GAN-toe-rap-tor

Gigantoraptor was not a true raptor. It was more closely related to the small Oviraptor (see pages 14–15). It was a speedy hunter of enormous size.

Professor Pete says:
This giant bird-like dinosaur was covered in feathers but, like ostriches today, it could not fly.

Gigantoraptor means 'giant thief'.

Gigantoraptor could probably run as fast as an ostrich, which can reach 64.4 kilometres per hour.

Gigantoraptor was about 8 metres long and weighed around 1.4 tonnes.

It lived in Mongolia during the Upper Cretaceous period, 85 Mya.

Gigantoraptor was a meat eater and hunted dinosaurs such as the small Protoceratops.

9

Microraptor

MIKE-crow-rap-tor

This tiny, feathered dinosaur had wing feathers on both its arms and its legs. Scientists think it spent most of its time in the trees. It glided from tree to tree looking for insects to eat.

Professor Pete says:
Microraptor used claws on its hands and feet to climb up tree trunks. It was safer from predators high up in the tree tops.

Microraptor means 'small thief'.

Microraptor had trouble running with its long leg feathers and probably could only manage a slow 12.8 kilometres per hour.

Microraptor was about 0.6 metres in length and weighed around 1.6 kilogrammes.

It lived in China during the Lower Cretaceous period, 130–125 Mya.

Microraptor ate insects.

Mononykus

mono-NIKE-us

Mononykus was a speedy little dinosaur with long legs and short arms which ended in a single claw. It was covered in feathers which were used for warmth and display.

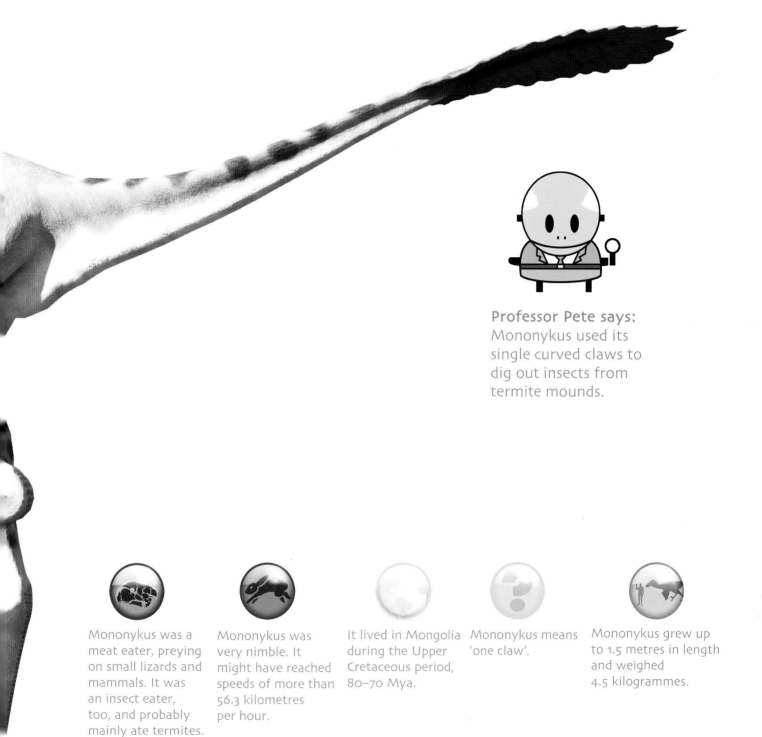

Professor Pete says:
Mononykus used its single curved claws to dig out insects from termite mounds.

Mononykus was a meat eater, preying on small lizards and mammals. It was an insect eater, too, and probably mainly ate termites.

Mononykus was very nimble. It might have reached speeds of more than 56.3 kilometres per hour.

It lived in Mongolia during the Upper Cretaceous period, 80–70 Mya.

Mononykus means 'one claw'.

Mononykus grew up to 1.5 metres in length and weighed 4.5 kilogrammes.

13

Oviraptor means 'egg thief'.

Oviraptor could probably run as fast as an ostrich, which can reach 64.4 kilometres per hour.

Oviraptor was about 2.1 metres in length and weighed around 25 kilogrammes.

It lived in Mongolia in the Upper Cretaceous period, 85–75 Mya.

Oviraptor was a meat eater and a **scavenger**, feeding on dead animals, clams and even raiding nests for eggs.

Oviraptor

OH-vee-RAP-tor

Oviraptor had an unusual appearance, very different from most dinosaurs. It had a bony crest and a strange-looking beak.

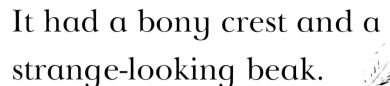

Professor Pete says:
Some scientists think the strange beak of Oviraptor was designed to crush the shells of clams so that it could eat them.

15

Therizinosaurus

THER-ih-zine-oh-SORE-us

This giant dinosaur had the
biggest claws of all. Although
they look like terrifying
weapons scientists think
they were used to drag
overhead branches towards its mouth.

Therizinosaurus was a plant eater.

 Therizinosaurus was too bulky to move fast. It probably managed a steady 8 kilometres per hour.

 It lived in Mongolia during the Upper Cretaceous period, 77–69 Mya.

 Therizinosaurus means 'scythe lizard'.

 Therizinosaurus grew up to 8 metres in length and weighed 3.6 tonnes.

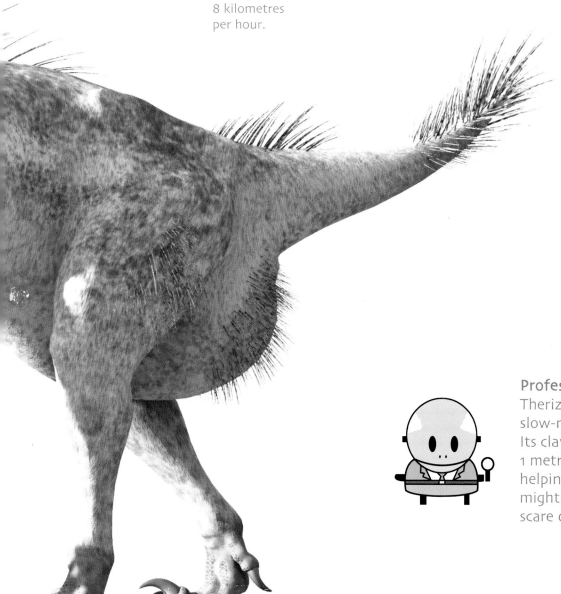

Professor Pete says:
Therizinosaurus was a slow-moving plant eater. Its claws were just under 1 metre long. As well as helping it to feed, the claws might have been used to scare off predators.

Troodon

TROH-oh-don

Troodon was one of the smartest
dinosaurs. It was fast and had
excellent vision so it might
have hunted at night. It had
large, killing claws on its
feet, which were raised
off the ground when running.

Troodon means 'wounding tooth' after its strangely **serrated** teeth.

 Troodon was fast. It could probably run up to 48.3 kilometres per hour.

 It lived in the United States during the Upper Cretaceous period, 74–65 Mya.

 Troodon was a meat eater.

 Troodon grew up to 2.2 metres in length and weighed 50 kilogrammes.

Professor Pete says:
Scientists have found evidence that it cared for its young after they hatched. This behaviour is rare among dinosaurs.

Utahraptor

yoo-tah-RAP-tor

This ferocious, speedy predator was armed with a 35-centimetre claw on one toe of each foot, claws on every finger of its hands, and razor-sharp teeth.

Utahraptor ate dinosaurs much larger than itself.

It lived in the United States during the Lower Cretaceous period, 112–100 Mya.

Utahraptor was 6 metres in length and 700 kilogrammes in weight.

Utahraptor was a fast heavy-weight but was not as speedy as smaller raptors. It ran up to 32.1 kilometres per hour.

Utahraptor means 'Utah's predator' because it was found in Utah in the United States.

21

Velociraptor ate insects, lizards and dinosaurs like Protoceratops.

 Velociraptor lived in Mongolia during the Upper Cretaceous period, 84–80 Mya.

 It measured up to 1.8 metres in length, and weighed up to 15 kilogrammes.

 Velociraptor might have had a fast top speed of 64.4 kilometres per hour.

 Velociraptor means 'speedy thief'.

Professor Pete says:
Hunting in packs, Velociraptors would have used tactics like lions do today to stalk and kill their prey.

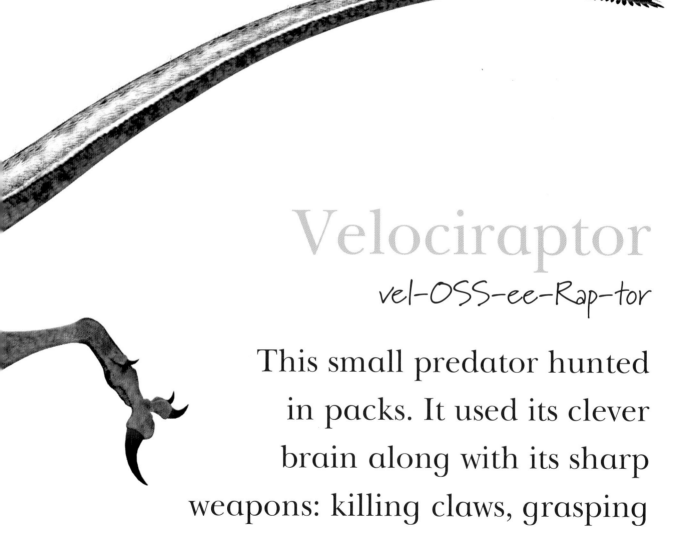

Velociraptor

vel-OSS-ee-Rap-tor

This small predator hunted in packs. It used its clever brain along with its sharp weapons: killing claws, grasping hands and needle-like teeth. It could bring down prey larger than itself.

Glossary

predator
An animal that hunts and kills other animals for food.

prey
An animal that is hunted by predators as food.

scavengers
Animals that feed on dead matter.

serrated
With a notched or saw-like edge.

Timeline

Dinosaurs lived during the Mesozoic Era which is divided into three main periods.

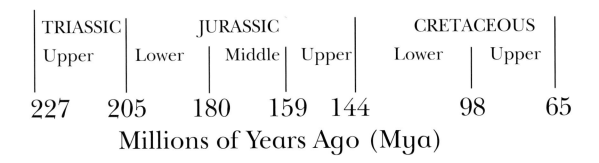

TRIASSIC		JURASSIC			CRETACEOUS	
Upper	Lower	Middle	Upper	Lower	Upper	

227   205   180   159   144   98   65

Millions of Years Ago (Mya)